C U T A W A Y
TRAINS

JON RICHARDS

COPPER BEECH BOOKS
BROOKFIELD, CONNECTICUT

© Aladdin Books Ltd 1998

Designed and produced by
Aladdin Books Ltd
28 Percy Street
London W1P 0LD

First published in the United States in 1998 by
Copper Beech Books,
an imprint of
The Millbrook Press
2 Old New Milford Road
Brookfield, Connecticut
06804

Editor
Simon Beecroft
Consultant
Tony Hall-Patch
Design
David West
Children's Book Design
Designer
Robert Perry
Illustrators
Simon Tegg & Ross Watton
Picture Research
Brooks Krikler Research

**Library of Congress
Cataloging-in-Publication Data**
Richards, Jon, 1970-
Trains / by Jon Richards ;
illustrated by Simon Tegg.
p. cm.
Includes index.
Summary: Presents different kinds
of trains, including steam trains,
diesel locomotives, and electric
monorails, and discusses how they
perform various jobs from carrying
cargo to moving people.
ISBN 0-7613-0824-5 (lib. bdg.).
— ISBN 0-7613-0743-5 (trHC)
1. Railroads—Juvenile literature.
[1. Railroads—Trains.] I. Title.
TF148.R52 1998   98-16915
625.1—dc21   CIP AC

CONTENTS

INTRODUCTION

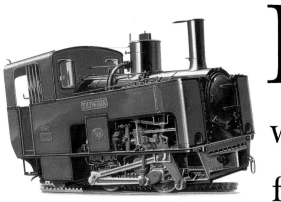

Before the arrival of cars and trucks, we used trains to travel from place to place.

We still use trains to get about, or to carry large loads of freight. But the puffing steam engines that once pulled the trains have been replaced by powerful diesel engines and very fast electric locomotives. Today, trains carry goods and people all over the world — some even run beneath our feet!

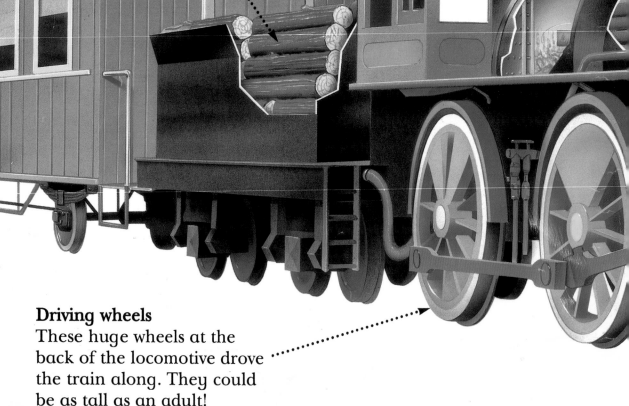

Tender
The small car behind the locomotive was called the tender. It carried the fuel for the fire and spare water for the locomotive.

Driver's cab
The driver's area on this locomotive was covered by a cab. This cab protected the drivers from the sun, the wind, and the rain.

Driving wheels
These huge wheels at the back of the locomotive drove the train along. They could be as tall as an adult!

EARLY STEAM TRAIN

This type of locomotive was used to pull passenger and freight trains during the early days of the American railroad.

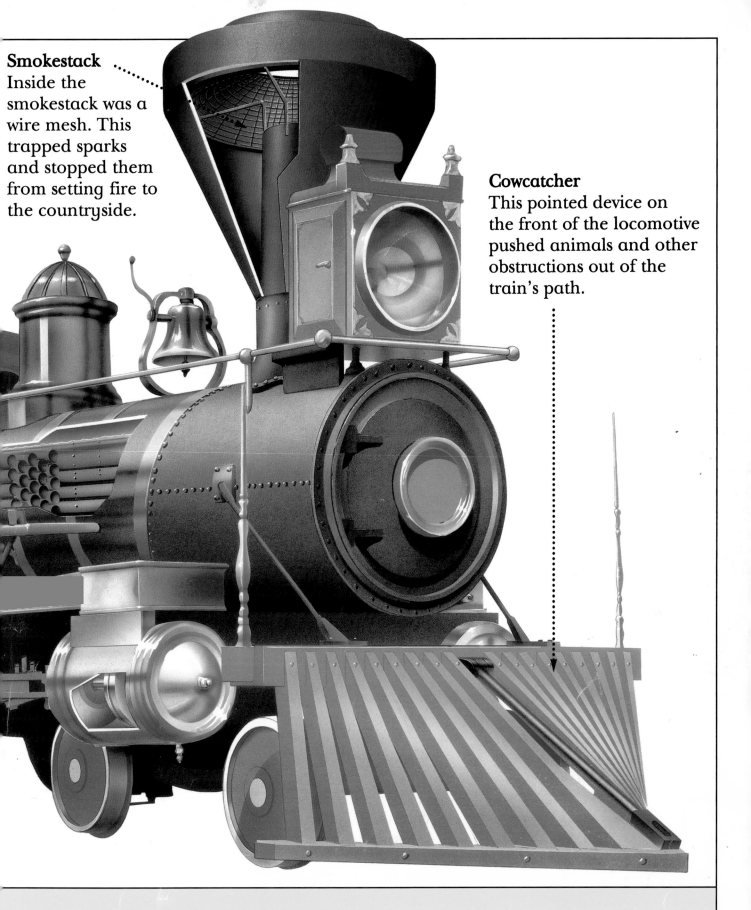

Smokestack
Inside the smokestack was a wire mesh. This trapped sparks and stopped them from setting fire to the countryside.

Cowcatcher
This pointed device on the front of the locomotive pushed animals and other obstructions out of the train's path.

It was called the 4-4-0 because it had four wheels at the front attached to a truck (*see* page 31) and four large driving wheels at the rear. It also had a "cowcatcher" on the front and a large, bell-shaped chimney called a smokestack.

It takes a lot of work

Crossing a continent

The first railroad to run across an entire continent was built in the United States. Two companies started building from opposite coasts. They met in the mountains of Utah in 1869 (*right*).

Bridges

Sometimes, railroads come across large obstacles such as lakes or rivers. To cross them, railroad builders construct bridges. These can be made from metal, stone, or even wood. This bridge (*below*) crosses the Forth River in Scotland.

to build a railroad.

Digging Tunnels

Another way to cross lakes and rivers and even mountains is by digging tunnels beneath or through them. This picture (*below*) shows the building of the world's longest rail tunnel. It runs under the sea between two islands in Japan.

Beating a path

If a railroad has to run through a forest, a path is cut through the trees (*left*). The wood from the cut-down trees can be used to build the tracks.

Chimney
The chimney at the front carries the heated air and smoke out of the locomotive.

Leading truck
The front four wheels are attached to a center pin, which allows the truck to swivel when the train takes curves in the track.

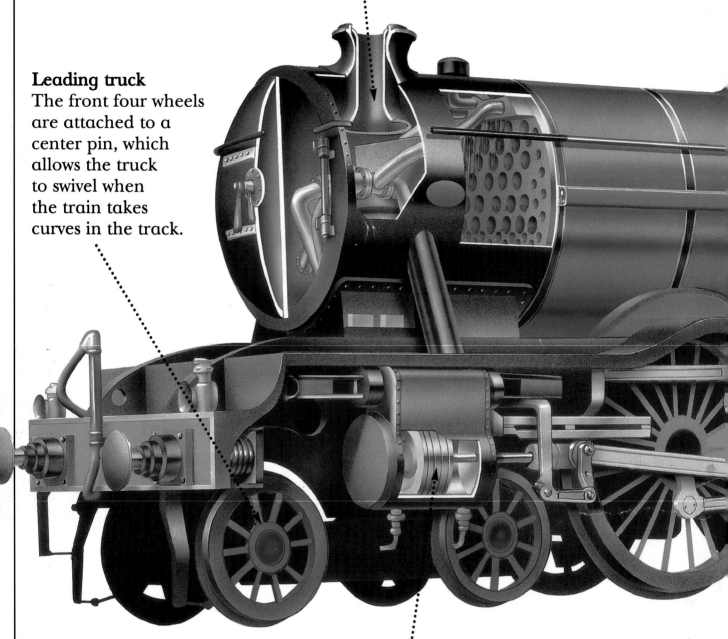

Pistons and connecting rods
Pressure from the steam pushes the pistons backward and forward. The pistons move the connecting rods that turn the wheels.

THE FLYING SCOTSMAN

The *Flying Scotsman* pulled passenger trains between England and Scotland beginning in 1922. Because it carried a spare crew and

Boiler
Tubes carry heated air from the firebox through the boiler. This heats the water inside the boiler until the water becomes steam — just like a huge kettle!

Firebox
Coal from the tender is shoveled into the firebox. Here, it is burned to heat the water in the boiler.

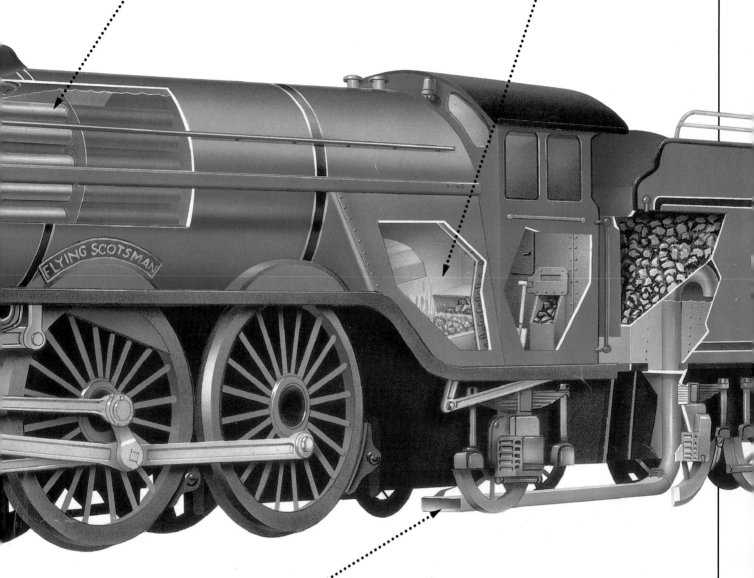

Water scoop
Rather than stop to collect fresh water, a scoop under the tender picks up water from a trough on the track as the train goes along!

picked up fresh supplies on the move, the *Flying Scotsman* could do the 393-mile (633-km) journey without stopping. Although steam trains are no longer used for everyday train travel in Britain, the *Flying Scotsman* still pulls the occasional special train.

Passengers on trains

Sleeping well

Many trains that travel through the night are fitted with sleeping compartments. In these, beds can be folded down to give passengers a good night's sleep (*left*).

Royal trains

When royalty use trains to travel from place to place, they do so in the utmost luxury. This passenger car (*below*) was used by Queen Victoria. The insides look more like a hotel than a railroad car!

can travel in luxury.

Freshen up

On the most luxurious train journeys, compartments may even have bathrooms (*right*). These help the passengers keep themselves clean.

Dining in style

Passengers on board some trains are treated to the best food. This is served at the tables by waiters (*below*).

Diesel engine
The Centennial locomotive has two powerful diesel engines to turn the electrical generators. Together, these engines are as powerful as 60 cars.

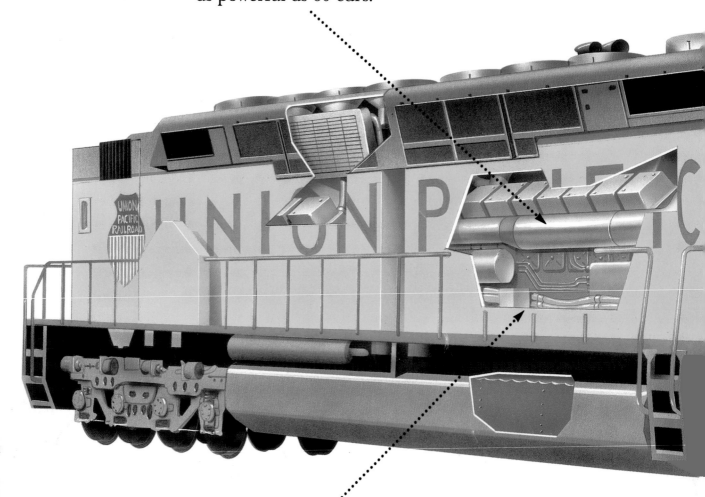

Quick starter
The crew on old steam trains need time to light a fire and heat the water in the boiler to make steam. A diesel-electric locomotive can be started a lot more quickly.

DIESEL-ELECTRIC
Diesel-electric locomotives use both diesel engines and electric motors to power them. This locomotive is the most powerful diesel-

Generators
When the generators are turned by the diesel engines, they produce electricity. This electricity powers the electric motors found in the trucks.

Coupler
Special couplers at the front and rear of the locomotive link it to the rest of the train.

Power unit
Each truck on this locomotive has eight wheels as well as the electric motors that turn them.

electric locomotive ever built. It is called a Centennial class locomotive, and was built for the 100th birthday of the Union Pacific Railroad company. Centennial locomotives were used to pull very long freight trains across the United States.

Not every train is

Big Boy

This locomotive (*above* and *below*) was the largest steam engine ever built. It was so long that it had to bend in the middle to get around corners. It was built to pull freight trains and it could pull a load that weighed the same as 2,000 elephants!

built to carry people.

Loading up

This freight train (*left*) has wagons that are filled with rocks that have been dug up from the ground. Some freight trains have flat cars to carry containers. Others have special cars that can carry automobiles.

Long trains

Freight trains are very long to carry as much cargo as possible (*above*). The longest freight train was 4.5 miles (7.3 km) long. It had 660 cars and needed 16 locomotives to pull it!

What it takes to

Fierce fire

Steam trains need a very hot fire to heat the water to make the steam. Here (*left*), the stoker is shoveling coal into the firebox to keep the fire burning fiercely.

Modern trains

Today, train drivers don't need to shovel coal to drive the train. Instead, they sit in a cab at the front of the train (*right*), controlling the train's speed.

drive a locomotive.

Come together

To make a long train, the wagons are joined together by hooks on their fronts and backs. These hooks are called couplers (*see* page 13). When the wagons are ready, a locomotive is added to pull the train along (*left*).

In control

A railroad system is controlled by computers from a central control room (*right*). Here, controllers can check on the progress of trains and make sure that they are traveling in the right direction.

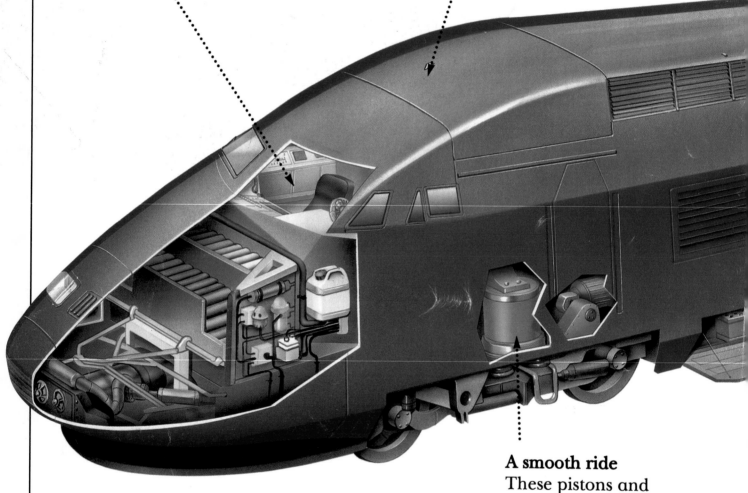

Driver's cab
From here, the driver controls the direction of the train, how quickly it accelerates, as well as the brakes that stop the train.

Go faster
To help the train go as quickly as possible, it has a pointed shape. This outline lets it travel through the air with the least effort.

A smooth ride
These pistons and springs make sure that the train rides smoothly over the tracks.

TGV

The TGV (Train à Grande Vitesse) is the world's fastest electric train and pulls passenger services throughout

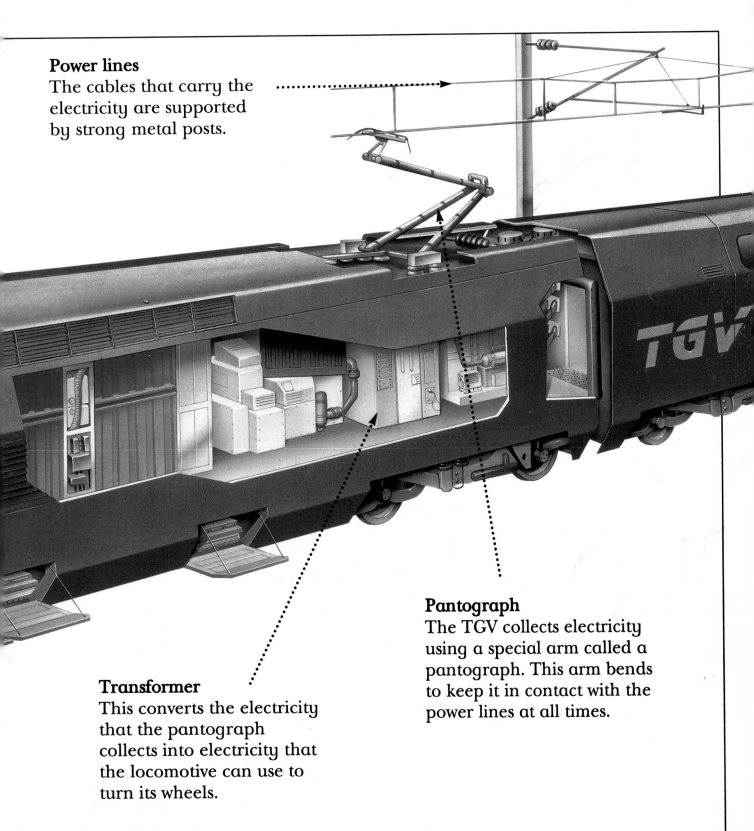

Power lines
The cables that carry the electricity are supported by strong metal posts.

Transformer
This converts the electricity that the pantograph collects into electricity that the locomotive can use to turn its wheels.

Pantograph
The TGV collects electricity using a special arm called a pantograph. This arm bends to keep it in contact with the power lines at all times.

France. It can fly along the track at a breathtaking 320 mph (515 km/h) — nearly twice as fast as a Formula One racing car! It is powered by electricity that it collects from power lines that run above the track.

Some trains are built

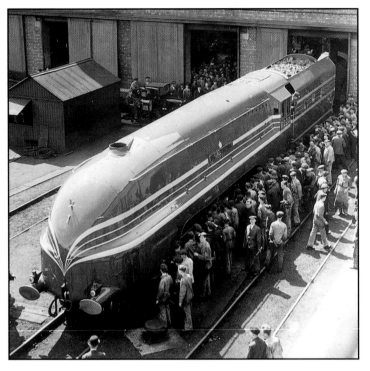

Fast steam

This steam train (*left*) was used in Britain during the 1930s. It was called a Coronation class locomotive. Its specially shaped body helped it to reach a top speed of 114 mph (184 km/h)! This was very fast for the time.

A speeding bullet

These trains (*below*) carry people in Japan. They were so fast when they were first used in 1964 that they were called "bullet" trains.

to travel very quickly.

European speed

This high-speed train (*above*) travels through Europe.
It is called ICE, which is short for Inter-City Express,
and it can zoom along at 206 mph (330 km/h).

Eurostar

This train (*right*) goes between
London and the cities
of Paris and Brussels.
It travels through the
Channel Tunnel
that runs under the
English Channel.
It can cruise along
at 180 mph (290 km/h).

SUBWAY TRAIN

Many cities around the world have large systems of underground railroads, or subways. The trains that run through these

Hanging around
This subway train is fitted with handles. People can hold on to these for support when they are standing up during their train journey.

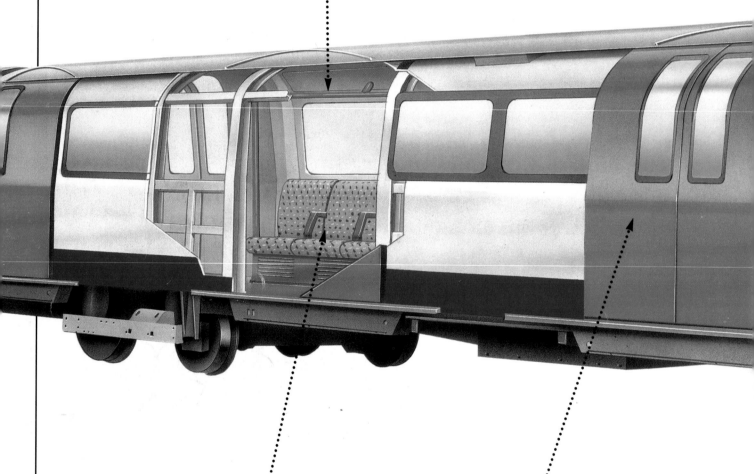

Take a seat
Passengers can sit down in seats that are lined up along either side of the train's cars.

Sliding doors
The doors on this subway train slide open automatically once the train has stopped at a station.

tunnels cannot be powered by steam or diesel because the fumes and smoke would stay trapped in the underground tunnels. Instead, they are powered by electricity, and pick up their power through "live" rails that run along the floor.

Driver's controls
One of the driver's controls is called a "dead-man's handle." If the driver lets go of this for any reason the brakes come on automatically and the train stops.

"Live" rails
Two of the four rails that this train runs on are called "live" rails. They carry the electricity that powers the train.

Some trains carry

Early subways

The first underground railroad ran beneath the streets of London (*above*). Since those early days, the London system has grown and now uses electric trains instead of the early steam locomotives. It has 255 miles (408 km) of track and 267 stations. Many of these stations are a maze of platforms, escalators, and tunnels (*right*).

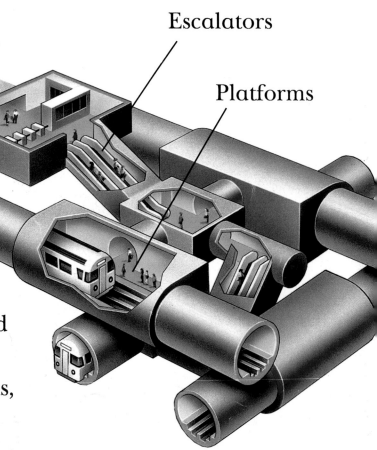

Escalators

Platforms

people underground.

Beneath the waves

The Channel Tunnel under the English Channel (*see* page 21) consists of two main tunnels and a central service tunnel (*right*). There are also emergency access tunnels running between them to let passengers escape from an accident.

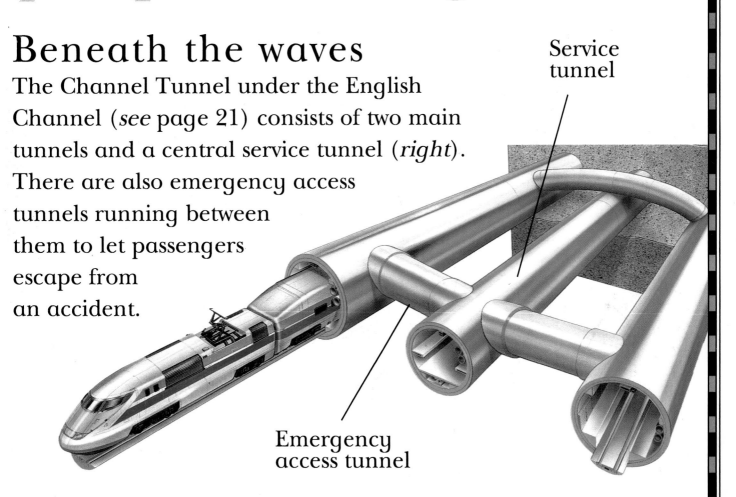

Service tunnel

Emergency access tunnel

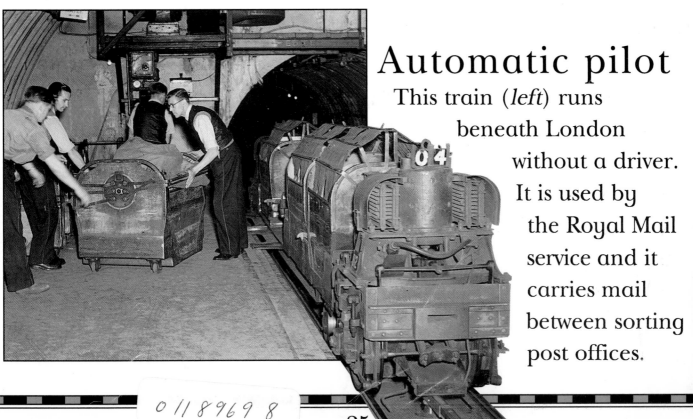

Automatic pilot

This train (*left*) runs beneath London without a driver. It is used by the Royal Mail service and it carries mail between sorting post offices.

0 1 1 8 9 6 9 8

Putting on the brakes

A maglev train doesn't have any brakes like a normal train. Instead, the force of the magnets under the train is reversed to bring it to a stop.

Passenger comfort

Because a maglev train does not run on rails, passengers enjoy a smoother and quieter ride than the ride on a normal train.

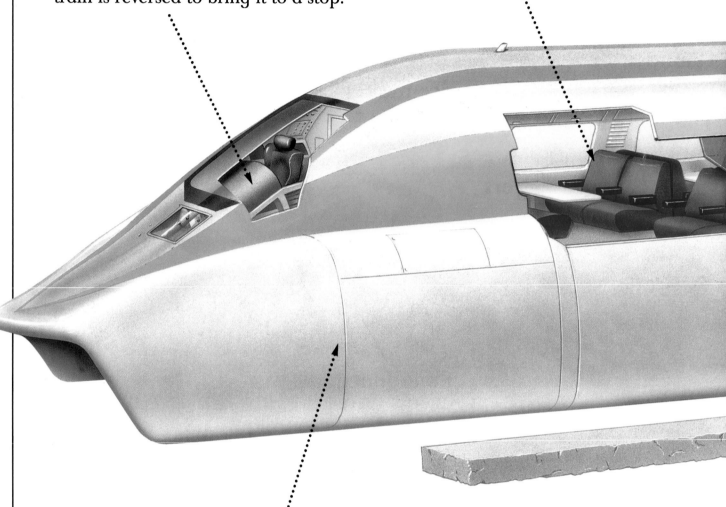

Zooming along

Maglev trains can reach very high speeds because they do not have to scrape along metal rails. Some of them can reach 315 mph (500 km/h)!

MAGLEV TRAIN

Instead of running on rails, a maglev (short for magnetic levitation) train actually floats above the ground!

Magnets

The magnets that make a maglev train float are found on top of the track and along the bottom of the train.

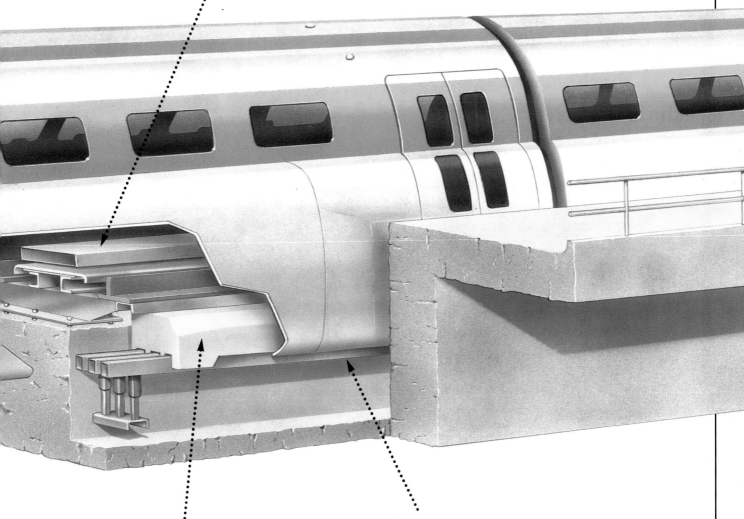

Keep it on track

Sets of magnets in the walls of the maglev track guide the train along the route as it moves.

Hovering

When it is running the body of the maglev train will float just 4 in (10 cm) above the track.

Special magnets run along the track and the train. These magnets produce forces that push against each other.

As these forces push against each other, the magnets are pushed apart and the train hovers above the track.

Some trains come

Mountain trains

Some trains run up the sides of mountains (*right*). To help them climb the steep slopes they have toothed wheels that pull the train up special middle rails.

Plane or train?

This experimental train (*right*) was pushed along by a huge spinning propeller. It could zoom along a monorail at 140 mph (220 km/h).

in unusual shapes.

City trains

Special short trains, or trams, run along tracks through the middle of some towns and cities (*right*). They help to reduce traffic congestion and pollution.

Monorail

Instead of running on two rails, some trains only use one rail. This one (*below*) travels on top of the rail — others may hang beneath it. These trains are called monorails.

Fantastic Facts

• The fastest steam locomotive in the world is called the *Mallard*. In 1938, it reached a speed of 125 mph (201 km/h) down Stoke Bank in the United Kingdom.

• The fastest vehicle ever run on a rail track was a rocket-powered sled. It reached a speed of 6,121 mph (9,851 km/h), or eight times the speed of sound. No one was on it at the time!

• The busiest underground railroad system in the world is the Greater Moscow Metro in Russia. It handles about 3.3 billion people every year!

• The United States has the greatest length of railroad track in the world. It has a staggering 138,666 miles (223,155 km) of railroad!

Train words

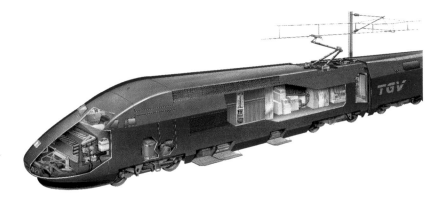

Boiler
The drumlike container on a steam locomotive where the water is heated and turned into steam.

Connecting rods
The rods that link the pistons to the wheels.

Cowcatcher
A pointed object on the front of a locomotive. It is used to push obstructions out of the train's path.

Firebox
Part of a steam locomotive where the fire is lit to heat the water in the boiler.

Locomotive
A self-propelling vehicle that is used to pull a train. It can be powered by steam, diesel, or electricity.

Stoking
Shoveling wood or coal into the firebox to fuel the fire.

Tender
The small wagon pulled behind the locomotive. It carries the fuel and water that the locomotive needs.

Truck
A wheeled trolley fitted to the bottom of a wagon or locomotive.

Index

PHOTO CREDITS
Abbreviations: t-top, m-middle, b-bottom, r-right, l-left, c-center.

Pages 4, 7b, & 17t – Corbis. 6-7, 8, 20t, 24, 25, & 28 – Hulton Getty Collection. 7m, 10, 11 both, 16 both, 18, 21 both, 26, & 29 both – Frank Spooner Pictures. 12, 14 both, 17b, & 20b – Solution Pictures. 22 – Paul Nightingale.

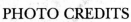